BATMAN, WHERE ARE YOU?

BATMAN, WHERE ARE YOU?

Ian Henery

Thynks Publications Limited

First published in 2012 by Thynks Publications Limited.

Registered Office:
White House, Clarendon Street, Nottingham, NG1 5GF England

http://www.thynkspublications.co.uk

Typesetting and Printing by
Book Printing UK
Remus House
Coltsfoot Drive
Woodston
Peterborough PE2 9BF.

ISBN: 978-1-900410-54-0

To my wife, Irene, who I truly do not deserve –
and my four beautiful daughters

PUBLISHER'S FOREWORD

It is a pleasure to publish Ian Henery's first collection of poems. He is a versatile poet who writes in a variety of styles and an even bigger variety of subjects. His poems range from being suitable for poetry in performance to those that fall easily on the page for contemplative reading. From haunting to happy, deeply thoughtful to wry and whimsical, it is befitting that Ian should be Poet Laureate to the Mayor of Walsall 2012/2013.

He is tireless in his support of worthy causes and five years ago he completed the 3 Peaks Challenge for Cancer Research. The following year he again completed the 3 Peaks Challenge for the British Dyslexia Association. He then contracted a viral infection which paralysed the left side of his diaphragm. This means he can only use one lung.

In 2009 and 2010, he attempted the Scout Chase Walk (40 miles in 16 hours) and managed to complete the Cotswolds Marathon with Gloucester Scouts. Last year, through the help of reflexologist, Clare Agg at Six Ways Clinic, he attempted the Scout Chase Walk again and completed 22 miles in 5 hours and raising money for a leper colony and orphanage in India. Ian is now receiving acupuncture treatment from Neil Quinton at Six Ways.

Recently, 6th Walsall Scouts, were burgled and lost £7,000 worth of kit, plunging them into doubt as to their future. Ian has already linked them up with Walsall Rotary & Walsall Rugby Club for a charity car wash AND tidying up after the V Festival at Weston Park (lots of camping gear left behind which they can keep). 2nd Walsall closed because of the lack of leaders. 6th Walsall have taken over their premises. Ian cycled 120 miles across the South Downs Way to raise funds to replace the lost equipment.

Proceeds from the sales of this book will go to the Mayor of Walsall's appeal for Leukemia Research.

i

PREFACE

I cannot imagine the pain of losing a child, much less watching a child (of whatever age) slipping away into the arms of death for want of medical care or funding into a disease that should be treatable. No child anywhere in the world should lose their life for want of medicine. Years ago I heard the curse (I cannot remember if it was a film or that I read it in a book): *May you outlive your children.* I didn`t understand at the time what it meant.

I shudder to think of the billions wasted on weapons of war: the nuclear arsenals that gather dust because no one dare use them while children starve in the dirt or die of malnutrion.

I would like to take this opportunity of thanking everybody who helped bring this project to fruition - Chris and Pam at Thynks Publications, Verity Edwards, the Mayor`s Secretary and the Walsall Mayor, Councillor Dennis Anson. His Appeal is Leukemia Research and this is a charity very close to his heart, since his daughter nearly died of the illness.

I also want to thank Claire Clews, who has helped me with PR and Krissy Griffiths, poet, workshop teacher and fine artist, who has designed the front cover of this collection. Thanks too to Pete Borlace, graphic designer, who has so generously contributed his skills free of charge for this project.

God bless to you all.
Ian Henery
Poet Laureate to the Mayor of Walsall 2012/2013

CONTENTS

BATMAN

Doesn't get his tights in a twist
Checking criminals on his list
It's Batman!

To him, Penguin is just a biscuit,
For Cat Woman, he'd risk it,
It's Batman!

He's the hero of the hour,
Makes the Joker cower,
It's Batman!

Who is Bruce Wayne?
Don't mention that name!
It's Batman!

Look! It's the Bat Light!
Watch the Riddler take flight!
It's Batman!

BATMAN, WHERE ARE YOU?

We urgently need you here,
Batman!
It's scary! There's much to fear!
Batman!

Cheryl Cole has gone to the States
Computers broken, can't get Bill Gates
Is this luck? Or is it fate?
Batman!

My little dog has run away,
Batman!
Tried to turn him vegetarian yesterday,
Batman!

My wife doesn't understand me!
The kids lock me in the lavatory!
Just want to retire by the sea,
Batman!

Want jeans with an elasticated waistband,
Batman!
And songs with lyrics I can understand,
Batman!

There are road works everywhere,
Smell of tarmac in the air;
It's in my clothes and in my hair.
Batman!

Where are you now, Dark Knight?
Look into the sky, see the Bat Light?
Rescue us, make everything right,
Batman!

There is apathy all around,
Batman!
The Euro is stronger than the Pound!
Batman!

We all want you as our Bat King,
Give Cat Woman your Bat Ring!
Peace and happiness you will Bat bring,
Batman!

BLACKBERRY PICKING

Purpley
    Abundantly
        Lovely
          Juicy

    Sweetly
        Lips Smackingly
        Down Throatery

Bouncy Bally
        From the parky
        Nicely
        Inside me.

CRINGE DRINKING

Binge drinking
It's cringe drinking.
Binge drinking,
Start thinking.
Stomach heaves, want to be sick,
Smell of vomit, head is thick.

Binge drinking,
It's cringe drinking.
Binge drinking,
Start thinking.
Smashed windows, children crying,
Hurt their mummy, feel like dying.

Binge drinking,
It's cringe drinking.
Binge drinking,
Start thinking.
Crashed my car, in a police cell,
Killed my passengers, going to Hell.

Date rape. Alcoholism. Ruined lives.
Hit the bottle, take a nose dive
Into the gutter, down the drain,
Only the pieces of puke remain.
Binge drinking,
Start thinking.
Cringe drinking,
Start thinking.

DIFFERENT LEVELS

Desperately trying to hold on,
Clinging to anything
                    Like a limpet
Just trying to believe.
Waves crash all around,
Dragging me back
And pulling me down.

Faith and courage rallies
And I spit out saltwater,
Wiping my eyes,
                    On a sodden sleeve.
Scrambling up a seaweed anchor,
Waves pounding in my ears,
Fingers scratching at rock
                    Breaking
Bleeding
For one small hope.

Useless.
Why force myself upon anything?

I release my grip,
Recede into the undertow
                    And become swamped
By laughing shingle
Before the wave crashes down.

In that instant,
I turn to see you,
Floating far away,
In a little boat.
You did not see me
Although I called your name.
I tried to reach out to you,
            But you faded away.
I was silenced by the waves' roar.

And the clattering shingle
Laughed.

FALLING LEAF

Let it go;
Release the grip
And submit
To the whim of change.

Life has its turns;
Nothing stays the same,
So you must adapt,
Always rebuilding.

Take the fall
                    Tumbling
Like a leaf
On the breeze.

Where you are bound
Depends on the flow
And
                    You.

GIRL IN A ROCKPOOL

Man in blue jeans and coat
Cries along the shoreline,
Followed by a little dog,
Blue and tan,
The concave bowl of the sky
Melted down to the sea,
Moulding the world in blue
Like his heart in a vice,
Squeezing the grief out
And rubbing the juice in his eyes.

Rock pools littered the beach,
Portals of nostalgia,
Like waves in a puddle of water,
Now the sea has gone.
Memories of family holidays
Cruelly reflected in mirrors
Of sky and water:
All blue
Tears flow and dog yaps
As man stumbled forward.

Picture this:
Blue moon in September,
Full with the bounty of harvest.
Turquoise sky pierced by stars,
Like opportunities still ahead of us.
Holding hands, returning indoors,
Framed by blue curtains,
Azure carpet
And walls the colour of powdered blue,
Flecked with white like wave-crests
The night of the diagnosis:
Ovarian cancer.

The bitter irony,
Cancer, your astrological sign
And mine the fish,
"We're two sea creatures
Frolicking beneath the waves."
Washed up here without you,
Crying into the spray,
Shouting over the surf
And cursing God across the water.
Can you hear me?

I fall, hoarse and exhausted,
My dog jumping the breakers.
Clutching the seaweed lip of a rock pool,
Red-rimmed eyes peer below,
Watching marooned marine life scuttle.
"Why you?" I scream,
Saltwater tears raining into the rock pool,
Vision blurred, I see your face,
Smiling back through the water,
Voice echoing in my head.

"I know that you loved me,
As I loved you.
We will meet again
In love;
Love is not changed in death,
Love lasts forever,
Always and eternal."
I sobbed,
As the image and voice
Faded.

HEART CRACKED OPEN

To taste the sweet thrill,
Of her,
And then tormented
By her absence.

To feel the tsunami of emotion,
Rising up,
Like a tempest,
Or a hurricane,
Only to plummet

Dead.
Nothing.
No future.
Facing the punishment
Of getting it wrong.
"There has been a misunderstanding."

She sits,
So innocent,
Smiling,
Watching you,
The way a vulture
Watches dying prey.

"There has been a misunderstanding",
She says,
And you feel,
As if you could die,
Heart cracked open.

HUSH, LITTLE ONE

The world grows still
And, one by one,
Wearied minds tired by day
Turn for retreat.
As clocks wind down.

A welcoming blanket
Wraps up the western sky
Perforated by stars,
Like tiny eyes,
Watching our slumber.

This is no time for worry;
Allow the merciful release
Cover your sleeping form,
Clothing you in dreams
And, in the fresh morn,

Rise like the sun,
Eager to begin again.
Know that Infinity's thread
Spins, weaves and ties us all
To this mortality.

Although I cannot see you,
Separated by Earthly distance,
And the vacuum of night,
You are with me now
As always;

In thought
And dreams
Sewn into the fabric
Of my person,
Bound in this incarnation.

Memories stir within my soul,
Recreating your human form,
Held close to my breast,
Feeling your heart beat
And kissing your eyes.

Sleep, my love
And in our dreams we shall be together
This night
And into Eternity.

IF I HAVEN'T GOT YOU

As I speed through a hectic life,
Working at police stations and Courts,
Grafting up to 12 hours a day,
Sometimes I forget I have a wife
As clients are in my thoughts
And staff I have to pay
                          But it means nothing
If I haven't got you.

A father with much responsibility,
Four daughters, needing love,
All the treasures this father needs;
It was you who gave them to me,
Gifts from God in Heaven above,
Strength when I'm on my knees
                          But it means nothing
If I haven't got you.

I look around at what I've got;
A home, car, law firm and stuff,
I can't take it with me when I die,
So you may as well burn the lot,
Your love for me is wealth enough,
I never want to say goodbye
                          It means nothing
If I haven't got you.

And I search for spiritual nourishment,
Attending courses, looking for God's law.
God is called by different names,
Like politicians sitting in Government,
It's a truth you can't ignore, '
God loves sinners all the same
                    It means nothing
If I haven't got you.

I'M A LITTLE POEM

I'm a little poem,
Never been to school;
Don't know much about exams
You might say I'm a fool.

I'm a little poem,
Don't have a posh uniform;
Not a member of fancy clubs,
Don't know how to conform.

> Got no mighty muscles,
> Got no towering voice.
> Deregulated in Brussels,
> No European Union choice.
> I'm outlawed and perverse,
> Never one for cliques.
> Sometimes defined as "verse,"
> Changing week by week.

I'm a little poem,
Elusive as a sprite.
Hard to see as a fairy,
Or a mole at midnight.

Where do I live?
Search for me in your soul.
What do I look like?
Individual voices in a choir,
Like sparks igniting a fire.

I NEED YOU

I need you,
Yes;
Effortlessly,
Without self-effacement
Or humiliation.
You are a childhood dream
Once lost and refound,
A secret I had forgotten,
The answer to my prayers.

And when I look at you
When the rage has subsided,
Like a stormy sea
Crashing against the shore,
Only to find peace
Again
And the shore
Unvanquished;
Like our love.

And I listen to you
Asking me why,
Why I love you so,
Why?
Why do I love you
More than myself;
Why would I tear my very soul
To make you mine?
Why?

How does a bird learn to fly?
Or a fish to swim?
Why do stars glitter?
And the Earth rotate?
Who tells the sun to shine?
And the moon to beckon tides?
What is the essence of life?
And the riddle of the Sphinx?
I do not know
Or care.
All I am aware
Is my need for you
Forever in my life
And, should our souls be willing,
Successive incarnations,
Alpha and Omega.

I THINK MY DAD IS BATMAN

My dad, he has special powers,
His smile can banish winter's showers;
But he has a secret, I am going to tell,
So listen hard and listen well;
I think my dad, I think my dad,
I think my dad is Batman!

Never seen him in tights and cape,
But there is no DIY he can't escape;
He says he is a night repairer of Church roofs
And changes his clothes in telephone booths.
I think my dad, I think my dad,
I think my dad is Batman!

Got legs that can't walk past pubs,
After he has dropped me off at Cubs;
Makes scale models out of coal,
And can even climb a telegraph pole;
I think my dad, I think my dad,
I think my dad is Batman!

The shed is really the Bat cave,
Robin is his best mate Dave;
I have never seen either in tights
Heading to the Bat Mobile at night:
But I think my dad, I think my dad,
I think my dad is Batman!

He knows the villains are at home
When he gets the call on the Bat Phone:
Poison Ivy, the Joker and Mr Freeze
Will beg for mercy on their knees;
'Cause I know my dad, I know my dad,
I know my dad is Batman.

LEAF

Candles flicker dim
While outside
Deformed angels,
In an abandoned graveyard,
Mock life's transience.
Covered with cobwebs,
Missing limbs, faces
And wings.
God's messengers point beguilingly
To roaming skies.

A little leaf
Falls,
Caught by the shifting breeze.
It's tiny weight
Is carried over the Earth;
Between boughs
Across fungi
And through protruding roots
Of erstwhile silent
Sentinels.

Leaf climbs,
Spiralling up airy staircases,
Surrendering to the whim,
Of change.
Sometimes, leaf settles
On rain-streaked grass
Before summoned,
Once again
And spun ever-onwards
In the breeze.

Nothing is forgotten
What once existed
Stirs within the loam,
Rejuvenating the Earth,
Whispering on the wind
And carried
In the creeping
Dark River.
Leaf dances,
Mindless to change.

LONDON DRY GIN

The early hours
And another bottle of alcohol.
Comforter, maternal teat,
"Whore's Drink";
Depressant.

Alone, listening to Jethro Tull.
Thick as a brick.
Spinning back down the years,
I remember,
London Dry Gin again.

Night. Locked out of home;
A labourer, now sacked,
Huddling for warmth,
Amongst lawn-mowers
In the garden shed.

Is it really 10 years since?
That night,
Climbing into rich people's gardens,
Feeding London Dry Gin
To wide-eyed goldfish.

MARILYN THE MERMAID

Marilyn the Mermaid
As sweet as can be;
Playing in the waves
And living in the sea.

A friend to the dolphins,
Beautiful seals and whales too
Together, just living a life,
In the peaceful ocean blue.

Pollution, death and misery,
Products of a superior race;
Hell-bent on destruction,
Pumping into the sea its waste.

Marilyn the Mermaid,
Crucified on the tuna nets;
Blown apart by fishermen
And condemned as a pest.

MY SPHELING (A reply to critiks)

Poor emblems of self,
Assorted paper and cheap pens
To plot life's curve,
In what I call Poetry.

Some inspired, some discovered.
(What is the difference?)
Tasting of experience,
Carrying meaning in the flow.

The essence of definition,
Fluttering across consciousness
Like a butterfly,
Awaiting the net.

Plucked, skewered still alive,
On a board, not for the squeamish.
Hoarded behind glass,
Visitors come to gape.

The mockery of exhibition,
Crucified and imprisoned,
Through guilt and pride,
Because of expression.

So what if I can't spell?
These leaking, imperfect
Words beg for benevolence
From kind-hearted editors.

NOT MINE

A beautiful face,
And a loving heart,
But not mine.

In this desert,
She is an oasis,
But not mine.

Days of conversation,
With only my thoughts,
But not hers.

An unbearable longing,
In tortured eternity,
But not hers.

Words cannot reveal,
The secrets in my breast.
I fear the devastation,

Confessions will reap.
Better to walk away,
And love the heart,

                  Not mine.

RHUBARB

Reddy, crunchy, not nicely
Unless it's sugary.
Sourary and big leafery,
Growing out of the earthery,
Smelly and dirtery.

Slugs and snails treatery
All slimy in the utility
And mashed and boiled
Perfunctory
Before crumblery or tartery

Poor rhubarb.

Loner of the fruit family.

SELF WORTH *(I am not a helpless petal for you to pluck)*

Loves me
Loves me not
Loves me
Loves me not
The bruises heal, but I've not forgot
The pain you put me through,
Covering my body black and blue.

Loves me
Loves me not
Loves me
Loves me not
And I see my baby in her cot
Blissfully asleep, safe and sound;
You will not crush her into the ground.

Loves me
Loves me not
Loves me
Loves me not
I look around and see what I've got,
Free from you, my own life,
Not buried in misery and strife.

I love me and I love you not
I love me and I love you
Not!

SOMEWHERE BEYOND

Echoes whisper
Somewhere down the wind
And waterfalls
   Tumble
To the Earth
  Drip
  Drip
  Drip
Sheepish clouds
Overarch the concave bowl
They call
       "the sky"
Our of here

And I think of you
Now
As always
         In all ways
Somewhere within
HERE.

SURRENDER

I love you,
Honest.
Doubting me
And all that we share,
Your tongue
Lashes over me
Like a bullwhip,
Flaying the skin
               Which covers
My pathetic form
Knelt in prayer.

Your eyes flash
As you sneer in disgust.
Musing over my grief,
You laugh,
As tongue slices open skin,
Keener than a razor
               Making me bleed
Before both your hands
Reach into me
Pulling apart fleshy folds
Mining for the agony.

I scream,
Watching my life-blood
Oozing between your fingers
And both your fists
Squeezing membrane and tissue.
Howling, I fight back,
Uselessly
As you rip me open,
Dissecting my brain
                    For curiosity
Or else sport.

I surrender.

TELEPHONE LINE

I miss you
Beyond words
And their clumsy,
Little definitions.

What can words say
But embarrassing clichés,
Or words that don't quite say
What you want them to say?

I miss you
And hardly say anything,
Instead, we both clutch plastic,
Feeling emotions together,
Crossing the empty void,
Two Gether,
Like One.

And I want to squeeze that plastic,
Yellow handset,
As if it were a banana
(Or else a lemon)
Until it burst
(So the pips popped)
Then you would feel
My overflow,
Oozing into your hand.
I could ooze buckets,
Towels would fill
And I would leak
All over the hallway
Perhaps lifeboats would be summoned,
And it would be all your fault,
For loving me.
(Although I love you more)

THE FAT & THE THIN

This is the fat poem:
He gobbles all the world's resources
And leaves nothing for others,
Not even his grandchildren.

This is the thin poem:
She always asks please
And says "thank you",
Even when the Fat Poem is mean,
Taking everything away,
From her.

This is the greedy Fat Poem:
Cutting downs rainforests
Polluting the oceans
Killing all the fish and animals
Just to eat more burgers
Build more takeaways
And cover all our countryside
In tarmac.

This is the Thin Poem:
Trying to stand up for herself,
Reminding everyone,
She is still there,
Like flowers
Growing between cracks in the pavement,
Promising summer blooms
In an asphalt world of grey
Concrete.

One day when the Fat Poem
Has gorged himself
Upon everything;
When polar bears and dolphins,
Elephants and the Ozone layer,
Are no more,
The Fat Poem will be sorry;

And the Thin Poem?
What do you say to bullies,
Thin Poem?
Rise up, frightened one,
Seize the keys to destiny
And say:

                    NO MORE!

TWINKLE TWINKLE LITTLE RABBIT
(for my daughters)

Celestial shafts of moonlight break the murky gloom,
Stopping their restricted time of earthbound perception.
Filtered diamonds enchant the world around this room,
Teasing the limitations of my airwaves' reception.
I finally feel that I can fly to you tonight
And opened windows to map the star-filled sky,
Clothing the world beneath its incandescent light
While the world dreamt, safe upon its sigh.

A voice echoed within my broken crystal radio:
"The Luminious Spacecraft leaves before the sunrise."
Pointing my telescope towards the starry halo,
I saw a smiling rabbit perced before my eyes!
The rabbit was seated upon a glowing crescent
And was laughing aloud as he waved down at me.
Starbound, he shot east towards the starry Levant,
Skimming over the waves of the sleeping sea.

WHERE DO I BEGIN? (*Dog Story*)
(*To be performed to the Theme Song of Love Story by Andy Williams*)

Where do I begin
To tell the story of how naughty a dog can be,
The story of my border terrier, Percy,
Who'd wag his tail whenever he saw me,
Where do I start?

With the first puppy bark,
Within my soul, there was a spark,
Imagined our life together at the park,
The place where our love story would start.

He fills my heart,
He fills my heart,
With new and varied things,
Chewed slippers and burst water wings,
A toy seen in practically everything.
A ruined lawn full of holes,
Burying the shoes he has stole,
This puppy thinks he's a mole!

Lawn is wrecked but I'm not lonely,
Is this how puppy ownership should be,
A dog who wags his tail with glee?
I reach for a paw, it's always there.

How long does this last
Before a shadow is cast
And this tale is in the past?
I have no answers now, but this much I can say,
Dog years are longer, any day;
I would never be alone, by myself,
A middle-aged man left on the shelf,
And he'll be there:

Jumping in the fish pond,
Urinating in my shoes,
Playing in the builders' sand
And running up and down the stairs.

YOU ARE

You are,
The first blush of a bride's cheek,
The promise of payday next week,
You are –

You are,
The first fluff on a young man's chin,
The hangover from a bottle of gin,
You are –

You are,
The knowing smile of first-conceived motherhood,
The fire that courses through my blood,
You are –

And when dreams are all around my feet,
Courage fails, heart misses a beat
Drowning, I'm lost in a storm,
Wondering who is keeping my bed warm,
You are –

And when the kids are all grown up,
Old, rationed to beer in an egg cup,
Deaf but never to an electric guitar,
Wondering who is waiting,
You are –